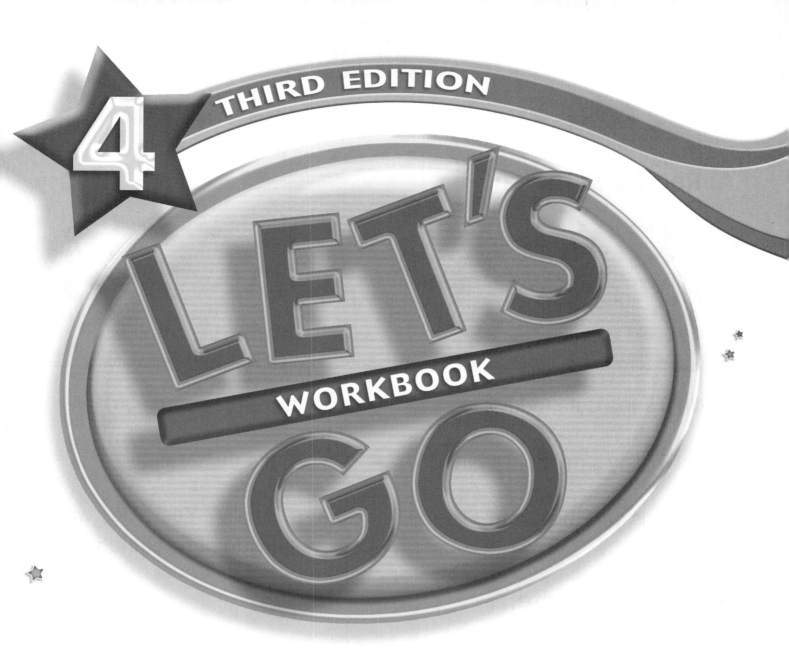

THIRD EDITION

4

LET'S GO

WORKBOOK

Christine Hartzler

Ritsuko Nakata

Karen Frazier

Barbara Hoskins

T0346859

OXFORD

UNIVERSITY PRESS

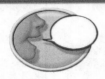

Let's Start

A. Read and match.

1. What's the date today? •

2. Oh! Today's my aunt's birthday. •

3. When is your birthday? •

• a. It's on August 3rd.

• b. It's the 21st.

• c. Really? Yesterday was my father's birthday.

B. Look and write.

When's your birthday?

1. Bob   <u>My birthday was</u> <u>three weeks ago.</u>

2. Julie   _____ _____

3. Tim   _____ _____

SEPTEMBER						
S	M	T	W	T	F	S
		1	2	3	4	5
6	7 Bob	8	9	10	11	12
13	14 Julie	15	16	17	18	19
20	21	22	23	24	25	26
27	28 Today	29	30 Tim			

C. Write.

1. 15 = _15th_

2. 4 = _____

3. 1 = _____

4. 23 = _____

5. 21 = _____

6. 7 = _____

7. 32 = _____

8. 12 = _____

9. 11 = _____

10. 29 = _____

11. 18 = _____

12. 26 = _____

D. Look and write.

April						
S	M	T	W	Th	F	S
1	2	3	4	5	6	7
8	9	10	11	12	13	14
15	16	17	18	19	20	21
22	(23)	24	25	26	27	28
29	30					

1. What's the date today?

   It's _the 23rd_____.

2. What was the date yesterday?

   It was _____.

3. What's the date going to be tomorrow?

   It's going to be _____.

December						
S	M	T	W	Th	F	S
						1
(2)	3	4	5	6	7	8
9	10	11	12	13	14	15
16	17	18	19	20	21	22
23/30	24/31	25	26	27	28	29

4. What's the date today?

   It's _the 2nd_____.

5. What was the date yesterday?

   _____.

6. What's the date going to be tomorrow?

   _____.

Let's Learn

A. Look and write.

had a party	drank hot chocolate	flew a kite
went to the store	met a movie star	took a test

1.

_____

2.

_____

3.

_____

4.

_____

5.

_____

6.

_____

B. Write.

1. take ⟶ <u>took</u>   2. go ⟶ _____   3. drink ⟶ _____

4. meet ⟶ _____   5. fly ⟶ _____   6. have ⟶ _____

C. Write the questions and answers.

1.

What did he do yesterday?

He flew a kite_____.

2.

What did she do yesterday?

_____.

3.

_____?

_____.

4.

_____?

_____.

D. Look, read, and check.

1. Did she go to the store?
   ☑ Yes, she did.   ☐ No, she didn't.

2. Did she have a party yesterday?
   ☐ Yes, she did.   ☐ No, she didn't.

3. Did he drink hot chocolate yesterday?
   ☐ Yes, he did.   ☐ No, he didn't.

4. Did he take a test yesterday?
   ☐ Yes, he did.   ☐ No, he didn't.

Let's Learn More

A. Unscramble, write, and number.

1. much too ate chocolate

   <u>ate too much chocolate</u>

2. race a won

   _____

3. a got present

   _____

4. money some found

   _____

5. phone lost his cell

   _____

6. broke window a

   _____

B. Write.

1. eat ⟶ <u>ate</u>   2. break ⟶ _____   3. get ⟶ _____

4. lose ⟶ _____   5. find ⟶ _____   6. win ⟶ _____

C. Look and write.

What happened?

1.  = She ate too much chocolate _____.

2.  = _____.

3.  = _____.

4.  = _____.

5.  = _____.

6.   = _____.

D. Write the questions and answers.

1.

What happened _____?

_____.

2.

_____?

_____.

Let's Build

Look and write.

Ben's Schedule

1. When did Ben find some money?

   He found some money on Friday the 7th_____.

2. What did he do yesterday?

   _____.

3. What's the date going to be tomorrow?

   _____.

4. What happened on Tuesday the 4th?

   _____.

5. What's the date today?

   _____.

6. What happened on Monday the 3rd?

   _____.

Let's Read

A. Write.

pancakes	Space Center	great	candles
tour	astronaut	parents	restaurant

1. My birthday was _____ this year.

2. First, my _____ and I went to a _____ for breakfast.

3. I had birthday _____ on my pancakes!

4. Then, we went to the _____ _____. I took a _____ and met an _____.

B. Read and check.

1. Abby's birthday was a lot of fun.

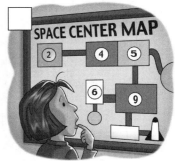

2. Abby took a tour at the Space Center.

Let's Start

A. Read and write.

> It isn't going to rain.   Should we take our jackets?
> It's going to be cold.   I'm really excited!

1. The school trip is tomorrow.
_____

Me, too!

2. What's the weather going to be like?

_____

3. _____

Yes, we should.

4. Should we take our umbrellas?

No, I don't think so.
_____

B. Read and circle.

1.

humid (hot)

2.

cool   warm

3.

foggy   hot

4.

cold   humid

C. Write the questions and answers.

1.

What's the weather going to be like tomorrow?

_____.

2.

What's the weather going to be like tomorrow?

_____.

3.

_____
_____?

_____.

4.

_____
_____?

_____.

✓

Let's Learn

A. Look and write.

a tent
sunglasses
a hat
a swimsuit
sunscreen
a towel
a sleeping bag
a flashlight

1. _____ 2. _____

3. _____ 4. _____

5. _____ 6. _____

7. _____ 8. _____

B. Read and write.

 He's going to go to the mountains.   She's going to go to the beac

1. _He should take a hat_____.   1. _She should take sunglasses___.

2. _____.   2. _____.

3. _____.   3. _____.

4. _____.   4. _____.

C. Look and write.

1.
She's going to go to the mountains.
She _should_ take a tent.
She _shouldn't_ take a swimsuit.
She _____ take a flashlight.

2.
He's going to go to the beach.
He _____ take a sleeping bag.
He _____ take sunscreen.
He _____ take a towel.

D. Look, read, and check.

1.
Should they take a tent?
☑ Yes, they should.
☐ No, they shouldn't.

2.
Should she take sunglasses?
☐ Yes, she should.
☐ No, she shouldn't.

3.
Should he take a towel?
☐ Yes, he should.
☐ No, he shouldn't.

4.
Should they take sunscreen?
☐ Yes, they should.
☐ No, they shouldn't.

Let's Learn More

A. Look and check. What do they have?

Max   Amy

Mary   Joe

	Max	Amy	Mary	Joe
a mitt	✓			
a bicycle				
a bucket				
a bat				
a tennis racket				
a fishing rod				
a tennis ball				
a helmet				

B. Look at A. Write sentences.

 1. He has a mitt and a bat _____.

 2. She has _____.

 3. _____.

 4. _____.

C. Write the questions and answers.

| play baseball | play tennis | ride a bicycle | go swimming |

1. What's she going to do?
   She's probably going to _____.

2. What's he going to do?
   He's probably _____.

3. What's he _____.
   _____.

4. _____.
   _____.

D. Look and write.

100% sure

1. She's __going to__ go fishing.

not 100% sure

2. He's __probably going to__ go hiking.

not 100% sure

3. They're _____ go swimming.

100% sure

4. They're _____ play tennis.

Let's Build

A. Read and write.

1. It's 7:45 a.m. She's probably going to _____

   _____.

2. It's 12:00 p.m. _____

   _____.

3. It's 4:00 p.m. _____

   _____.

4. It's 10:00 p.m. _____

   _____.

go to school
go to bed
eat lunch
do homework

B. Look and answer the questions.

1.

What's the weather going to be like?

_____.

Should he take his jacket?

_____.

What else should he bring?

_____.

2.

What's the weather going to be like?

_____.

Should they bring sunglasses?

_____.

What else should they bring?

_____.

Let's Read

A. Read and write.

> indoors   third   second   shine
> mirror   first   lights   rainbow

1. You can make a rainbow _____.
_____, put water in a glass.

2. _____, put a small _____ inside the glass and tilt it up slightly.

3. _____, turn off the _____.

4. _____ a flashlight onto the mirror.
You're going to see a _____ on the wall!

B. Answer the questions.

1. Should you use a mirror?

_____.

2. Should you put water in a bucket?

_____.

3. Should you turn off the lights third?

_____.

4. Should you shine a flashlight on the wall?

_____.

Units 1-2 Listen and Review

A. Read and connect.

1. The school trip is tomorrow. •

2. What's the date today? •

3. What's the weather going to be
   like tomorrow? •

4. My birthday was three weeks ago. •

• a. I didn't know that!
   Happy birthday!

• b. It's going to be cold.

• c. I'm really excited!

• d. It's the 21st.

B. Write the questions.

1.

_____?

They're probably going to have
a party.

2.

_____?

He's probably going to fly a kite.

C. What about you? Write.

1. What was the date yesterday? _____

2. When's your birthday? _____

3. What did you do yesterday? _____

4. What are you going to do on Sunday? _____

CHRIS AND CINDY'S TREASURE HUNT

Part One

A. Read and check.

1. "We're going to go on a treasure hunt!" said Aunt Angie.

2. Aunt Angie had the first clue for the treasure hunt.

3. It's not a beach, but there's a lot of sand. You should take your hats and sunscreen.

4. Uncle Al is holding your next clue in front of a big triangle.

B. Answer the questions.

1. What are they going to do?

_____.

2. Who is Angie?

_____.

3. What should Chris and Cindy take?

_____.

4. Where is Uncle Al?

_____.

✓

Unit 3 Hopes and Dreams

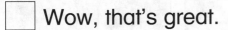 Let's Start

A. Read and number.

☐ Wow, that's great.

☐ What about you, Scott?

1 What do you want to be?

☐ No, I don't. I want to be a singer.

☐ I want to be rich!

☐ Do you want to be an astronaut, too?

☐ I want to be an astronaut.

B. Read and match.

1. a musician •

2. a news reporter •

3. a writer •

4. a scientist •

5. an astronaut •

6. a singer •

C. Write the questions and answers.

1. What do you want to be ?

I want to be a singer .

2. _____?

_____.

3. _____?

_____.

4. _____?

_____.

D. What about you? Write.

What do you want to be?

_____

Let's Learn

A. Look and write.

1.
2.
3.

1. She wants to be a ___tour guide___.

   She doesn't want to be a _____.

2. _____.
   _____.

3. _____.
   _____.

| flight attendant | architect | delivery person |
| truck driver | pop idol | tour guide |

B. Read and check.

1.  She doesn't want to be a delivery person.

   ☐ True ☐ False

2.  He wants to be an architect.

   ☐ True ☐ False

C. Write the questions and answers.

1.

What does he want to be?

_____.

2.

_____?

_____.

3.

_____?

_____.

4.

_____?

_____.

D. Look at C. Answer the questions.

1. Does he want to be a pop idol? _Yes, he does_____.

2. Does she want to be an architect? _____.

3. Does she want to be a flight attendant? _____.

4. Does he want to be a truck driver? _____.

Let's Learn More

A. Read and match.

1. design a video game •

2. climb a mountain •

3. drive a car •

4. sail a boat •

5. travel around the world •

6. build a house •

B. Look and write.

1.

   She wants to _____.

   She doesn't want to _____

   _____.

2.

   _____.

   _____

   _____.

C. Connect and write the questions and answers.

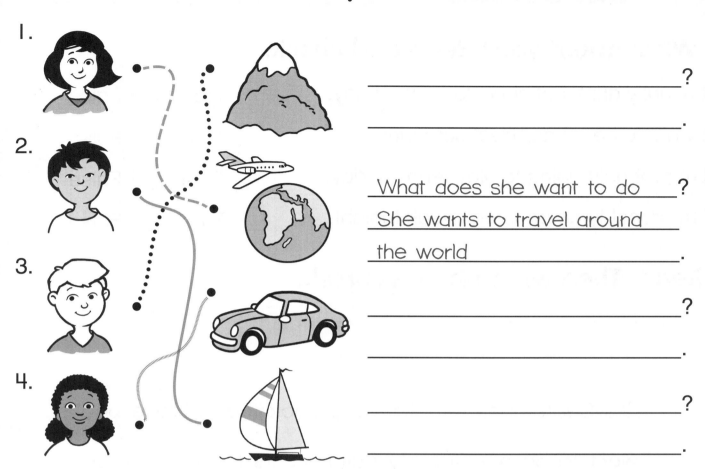

1.

_____?

_____.

2.

What does she want to do   ?

She wants to travel around

the world   .

3.

_____?

_____.

4.

_____?

_____.

D. Read and check.

1. Does she want to build a house?

☐ Yes, she does.
☐ No, she doesn't.

2. Does he want to travel around the world?

☐ Yes, he does.
☐ No, he doesn't.

3. Does he want to climb a mountain?

☐ Yes, he does.
☐ No, he doesn't.

✓

Let's Build

A. What about you? Read and check.

1. I usually drink hot chocolate every day. ☐ True ☐ False

2. I want to be an architect someday. ☐ True ☐ False

3. I'm probably going to play tennis today. ☐ True ☐ False

4. I'm probably going to eat steak tonight. ☐ True ☐ False

B. Read. Then write about yourself.

> It's September 10th. I read a book today. I love books!
>
> I want to be a writer. My sister wants to be a doctor.
>
> I don't want to be a doctor! I want to travel around the
>
> world and write.

It's _____. I _____ today. I love _____!

I want to be a _____. My _____ wants to be a

_____. I don't want to be a _____! I want to

_____ and _____.

Let's Read

A. Read.

1.

Anna Johnson is a volunteer at the zoo. She likes to work with animals. She works with dolphins every day. She feeds them every morning and helps train them, too. Someday Anna wants to be a dolphin trainer.

2.

Teri is Anna's sister. She is a volunteer at the hospital. She doesn't want to work with animals. She likes to help people. She wants to be a nurse someday.

B. Read A. Fill in the chart.

	Name: _____	Name: _____
Who?		
What?		
Where?		
Wants to be?		
Why?		

✓

 **Let's Start**

A. Unscramble and write.

1.

subject your What's favorite?

_____

I like science.

2.

like Why you do it?

_____

I think it's easy.

3.

best subject you like Which do?

_____

I like English. It's easier than science.

B. Read and write.

| think | easy | science | hard |

1. Why do you like _____?

2. I think it's _____.

3. I don't think so. I _____ it's _____.

C. Write the words.

Down

1.

2.

3.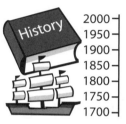

4.

Across

5.

6.

D. Complete the questions and answers.

1.  What's your favorite subject?

   I like literature

   _____.

2.  What's your

   _____?

   _____

   _____.

3.  _____

   _____?

   _____

   _____.

4.  _____

   _____?

   _____

   _____.

Let's Learn

A. Look, read, and match.

1.

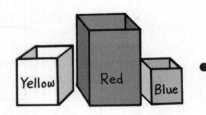

•   • The red box is smaller than the yellow box.
The blue box is the smallest.

2.

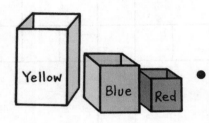

•   • The blue box is bigger than the red box.
The yellow box is the biggest.

3.

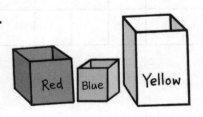

•   • The yellow box is smaller than the red box.
The blue box is the smallest.

B. Write.

1. big ⟶ <u>bigger</u> ⟶ <u>the biggest</u>

2. short ⟶ _____ ⟶ _____

3. light ⟶ _____ ⟶ _____

4. long ⟶ _____ ⟶ _____

5. heavy ⟶ _____ ⟶ _____

6. small ⟶ _____ ⟶ _____

C. Write the questions and answers.

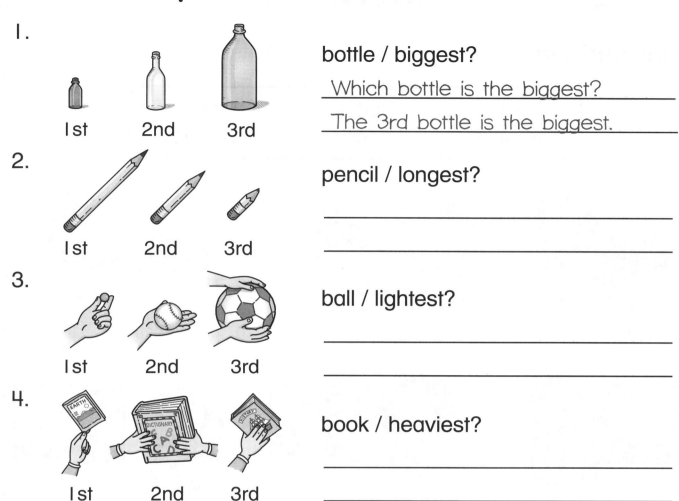

1.
1st   2nd   3rd

bottle / biggest?

Which bottle is the biggest?

The 3rd bottle is the biggest.

2.
1st   2nd   3rd

pencil / longest?

_____

_____

3.
1st   2nd   3rd

ball / lightest?

_____

_____

4.
1st   2nd   3rd

book / heaviest?

_____

_____

D. Look and write.

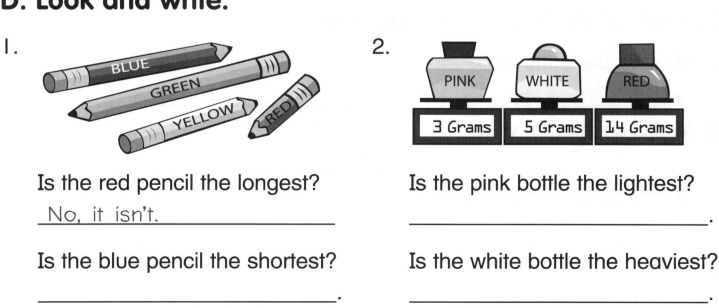

1.
BLUE
GREEN
YELLOW   RED

Is the red pencil the longest?

No, it isn't.

Is the blue pencil the shortest?

_____.

2.
PINK   WHITE   RED
3 Grams   5 Grams   14 Grams

Is the pink bottle the lightest?

_____.

Is the white bottle the heaviest?

_____.

A. Look and write.

bad	better	worse
the best	good	the worst

1. ___bad___

2. _____

3. _____

4. _____

5. _____

6. _____

B. Look at A. Answer the questions.

1. Which cake is the best?

   Ray's cake is the best _____.

2. Which cake is the worst?

   _____.

3. Which picture is the worst?

   _____.

4. Which picture is the best?

   _____.

C. Read and answer the questions.

	Talent Show	Points
Matt	Dancing	5
	Singing	8
	Cooking	10
Lina	Dancing	9
	Singing	4
	Cooking	3
Carl	Dancing	6
	Singing	10
	Cooking	7

1. Who's the best singer?
   <u>Carl is the best singer</u>.

2. Who's the best dancer?
   _____.

3. Who's the worst cook?
   _____.

4. Who's the worst dancer?
   _____.

Lina

Matt

Carl

D. Look at C. Read and check.

1. Is Matt a better cook than Carl?   ☑ Yes, he is.   ☐ No, he isn't.

2. Is Carl a better cook than Lina?   ☐ Yes, he is.   ☐ No, he isn't.

3. Is Lina a worse dancer than Carl?   ☐ Yes, she is.   ☐ No, she isn't.

4. Is Lina a worse singer than Carl?   ☐ Yes, she is.   ☐ No, she isn't.

Let's Build

A. Look and make sentences.

1.

long

English class is longer than

_____.

Science class is _____.

2.

short

_____.

_____.

3.

Steve   Jen   Andy

good

_____.

_____.

4.

white   yellow   orange

heavy

_____.

_____.

B. What about you? Write.

1. What's your favorite subject? _____.

2. Why do you like it? _____.

3. What's your favorite sport? _____.

4. Why do you like it? _____.

Let's Read

A. Look and write.

| falcon | sailfish | swan | whale |

1. _____ 2. _____ 3. _____ 4. _____

B. Look and write.

| in the air | in water | on land |

1.
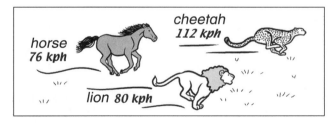

The _____ is the fastest animal _____.

2.

The _____ is the fastest animal _____.

3.

The _____ is the fastest animal _____.

Units 3-4 Listen and Review

A. Read and connect.

1. She wants to be a flight attendant. •

2. She wants to be an architect. •

3. She wants to be a scientist. •

4. She wants to be a news reporter. •

• She wants to be on TV.

• She wants to travel around the world.

• She wants to build a house.

• She thinks science is easier than English.

B. Read and check.

1. He thinks literature is hard.

2. She thinks geography is harder than history.

3. Hal's house is worse than Hannah's house.

4. Nina's cookies are good, but Jenny's cookies are better.

CHRIS AND CINDY'S TREASURE HUNT

Part Two

A. Look and write.

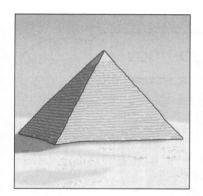  

Egypt

The Great Pyramid

kids

1. _____ 2. _____ 3. _____

B. Read, write, and number.

☐ Find the biggest _____ and _____ in front of it.

☐ "Hi, kids!" he said.
"Hi, Uncle Al. Do you have our _____ clue?" asked Cindy.
"Yes, I do," he said. "_____ it is."

☐ "This _____ is harder," said Cindy.
"But I _____ I know," said Chris.

1 "Egypt is _hot_!" said Chris. "_____," said Cindy.
"_____ the Great Pyramid."
"And there's Uncle Al with three water _____!" said Chris.

Look
hot
next
Here
waterfall
bottles
think
clue
ride a boat
There's

✓

Let's Start

A. Look and circle.

1.

How was the show?

FUNLAND PRESENTS

It was really fun.
I'm so excited!

2.

Where are you now?

We're at the roller coaster.
We want to go on the roller coaster, too.

3.

Can you wait for us?

Sure. But hurry!
We're waiting in line.

4.

Thanks for waiting for us.

I'm so excited!
No problem.

B. Unscramble and write.

1.

redbo

_____

2.

sedprisur

_____

3.

deirrow

_____

4.

treesdeint

_____

5.

cixeedt

_____

6.

radasrembes

_____

C. Look and write.

1.

THEATER
Big Show Tonight!

I'm _____ !

Me, too !

2.

They're _____ .

_____ .

Let's Learn

A. Write and number.

> visited   downloaded   played
> listened   practiced   watched

1. _____ a baseball game   4. _____ to the radio

2. _____ music   5. _____ the violin

3. _____ their grandparents   6. _____ a board game

B. Look and write sentences.

1.

They _____ last week.

2.

He _____ yesterday.

C. Write the questions and answers.

yesterday

last week

three months ago

last year

1. What did they do <u>three months ago</u>?

   <u>They watched</u>_____.

2. What did she do _____?

   _____.

3. _____?

   _____.

4. _____?

   _____.

D. Read and circle.

1. Did she listen to the radio?

   Yes, she did.

   (No, she didn't.)

2. Did he play a board game?

   Yes, he did.

   No, he didn't.

3. Did they play the violin?

   Yes, they did.

   No, they didn't.

4. Did they download music?

   Yes, they did.

   No, they didn't.

Let's Learn More

A. Look and write the letter.

1. up _____

2. down _____

3. around _____

4. through _____

5. over _____

6. under _____

7. into _____

8. out of _____

a   b   c   d

e   f   g   h

B. Circle.

1. He went (into / out of) the woods.

2. They went (up / down) a hill.

3. She went (through / over) a tunnel.

4. He went (around / under) a bridge.

C. Look and write.

1.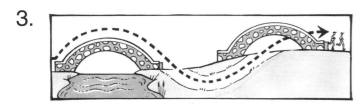

She went _____

and _____.

2.

He went _____

and _____.

3.

They went _____

and _____.

D. Complete the questions and answers.

1. Where did __the bird__ go?

   __It went__ into the barn.

2. Where did _____ go?

   _____ under the car.

3. Where did _____ go?

   _____ up a tree.

4. Where did _____ go?

   _____ into the pond.

Let's Build _____

A. Make sentences.

1. she / French fries / this morning _____.

2. they / museum / last weekend _____.

3. he / roller coaster / yesterday _____.

4. she / sandwich / last night _____.

B. Look at A. Write questions.

1. What _____?

2. Where _____?

3. What _____?

4. What _____?

C. Answer the questions.

What about you?

1. What did you eat for breakfast today?

   _____.

2. Who did you eat breakfast with today?

   _____.

3. Where did you eat breakfast today?

   _____.

4. When did you eat breakfast today?

   _____.

Let's Read

A. Read and match.

Dear Joey,

1. We are having fun in Australia! •

2. Uncle Mark and I went to the wildlife park yesterday. I fed a kangaroo and held a koala. •

3. Uncle Mark went through the reptile house and fed a crocodile. He looked scared! •

4. Tomorrow we are going to go sailing. •

                    Aunt Tina

B. Answer the questions.

1. Who looked scared? _____.

2. Who held a koala? _____.

3. Where are Aunt Tina and Uncle Mark? _____.

4. When are they going to go sailing? _____.

 # Let's Start

A. Read and number.

[ ] What does she look like?

[ ] Yes, it is. Thanks!

[ ] Who are you looking for?

[ ] She has short red hair and green eyes.

[1] Can I help you?

[ ] I'm looking for my aunt.

[ ] Yes, thanks. I'm looking for someone.

[ ] Is that her over there?

B. Match.

1. one person •   • no one

2. no people •   • everyone

3. all people •   • someone

C. Read and write the letter.

1. Can I help you?
   Yes, thanks. _____

2. Can I help you?
   No, thanks. I'm OK. _____

a.    b.

D. Write.

1. mother = <u>mom</u>

2. father = _____

3. grandmother = _____

4. grandfather = _____

E. Look and write.

aunt   uncle   cousin   sister   mom   dad

Who are you looking for?

1.

<u>I'm looking for my aunt</u>.

2.

_____ <u>my dad</u>.

3.

_____.

4.

_____.

5.

_____.

6.

_____.

Let's Learn

A. Look, read, and circle.

1.

   1. He has (curly) / straight hair and a beard. / moustache.

2.

   2. She has short / curly hair and bangs. / a ponytail.

3.

   3. He has a moustache / beard and long / straight hair.

4.

   4. She has curly / straight hair and a ponytail. / bangs.

B. Look at the chart. Circle True or False.

	Eye color	Hair style	Hair color
Joe	green	straight	brown
Paul	brown	curly	red
Liz	blue	long	blond
Tina	black	bangs	black

1. Liz has blond hair and brown eyes.
   True   (False)

2. Joe has green eyes and brown hair.
   True   False

3. Paul has blond hair and brown eyes.
   True   False

4. Tina has black hair and bangs.
   True   False

C. Write the question or answer.

Maxine's Photos

Mom and Dad

Grandma and Grandpa

Cousin Sal and Uncle Jim

My sister and me

1. What does Maxine's mom look like?

   _____.

2. What does her sister look like?

   _____.

3. What does her uncle look like?

   _____.

4. _____?

   He has a moustache and curly hair.

5. _____?

   He has gray hair and a moustache.

6. _____?

   He has blond hair and a beard.

✓

Let's Learn More

A. Find and circle the words. Then label the pictures.

k	e	r	s	i	e	t	m	n	q	r	s
a	g	c	f	l	v	e	s	t	o	z	n
r	l	m	g	b	a	c	p	q	l	f	e
b	a	s	e	b	a	l	l	c	a	p	a
n	s	e	a	l	b	p	s	v	i	m	k
n	s	o	t	o	h	s	h	e	t	o	e
t	e	b	s	u	i	t	w	y	u	o	r
i	s	v	e	s	s	a	n	d	a	l	s
e	a	b	g	e	t	h	e	w	f	j	k

1.

a _____

2.

a _____

3.

a _____

4.

a _____

5.

a _____

6.

_____

7.

_____

8.

_____

B. Complete the sentences.

1.

The man is _____ wearing a vest.

2.

The boy _____

_____ .

3.

The girl _____

_____ .

4.

The woman _____

_____

C. Write the questions.

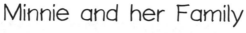
Minnie and her Family

| Minnie's older brother, Milt | Minnie's younger sister, Marie | Minnie | Minnie's older sister, Mary | Minnie's father, Max |

1. Which girl is Minnie's older sister _____?
   She's the girl with long, straight hair and bangs.

2. _____?
   She's the girl in a polka-dot dress and sandals.

3. _____?
   He's the boy in pants and a plaid shirt.

4. _____?
   He's the man in pants and a T-shirt.

D. Write the answers.

1. Which dog is Milt's dog?

   It's the dog with _____ hair.

2. Which dog is Minnie's dog?

   _____.

Let's Build

A. Look at the chart. Complete the sentences.

	Hair style	Hair color	Eye color	Face	Clothes
Ted	straight	brown	green	beard	tie
Molly	ponytail	red	blue		blouse
Sid	curly	black	black	moustache	vest
Jane	bangs	brown	blue		sandals

1. Sid is the man with _____, _____ hair and _____ eyes. He has a _____. He's wearing a _____.

2. Jane is the girl with _____ and _____ hair. She has _____ eyes. She's wearing _____.

3. Ted is the man with _____, _____ hair and _____ eyes. He has a _____. He's wearing a _____.

4. Molly is the woman with _____ hair and a _____. She has _____ eyes. She's wearing a _____.

B. Look at A. Write the names.

1. _____   2. _____   3. _____   4. _____

Let's Read

Look, read, and write.

powder	a piece of tape	mirror
lotion	fingerprint	lift

Let's Make a Fingerprint!

☐ Then, touch a _____.

☐ _____ the tape and put it on a piece of black paper.

1 First, put _____ on your hands.

☐ Put _____ on the mirror.

☐ Brush the powder away.

☐ Then you can see your _____.

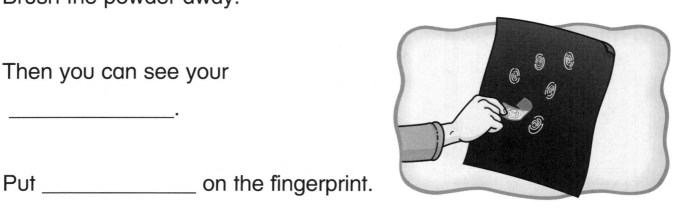

☐ Put _____ on the fingerprint.

Units 5-6 Listen and Review

A. Read and connect.

1. What did you do last night? •   • She has straight black hair.

2. Where did the cat go? •   • I'm looking for my brother.

3. Which cat is Pearl? •   • He went over the bridge and around the pond.

4. Where did he go? •   • The cat went up a tree.

5. Who are you looking for? •   • I downloaded music.

6. What does she look like? •   • Pearl is the cat with green eyes.

B. Look and write.

Tom, two weeks ago

Anna, yesterday

1. What does Tom look like?

   He has _____, _____ hair

   and a _____.

2. What did he do two weeks ago?

   He _____.

3. What does Anna look like?

   She has _____ hair and

   a _____.

4. What did she do yesterday?

   She _____.

CHRiS AND CiNDY'S TREASURE HUNT

Part Three

Read and circle.

1. "Iguazu Falls is beautiful!" said Cindy.

   "But I'm ⟨cold!" / wet!"⟩ said Chris.

2. "Are you Chris and Cindy?" asked a man.
   "Yes, we are!"

   "Here's your clue," / cave," said the man.

3. This place is in the beach, / desert, but it's always warm. / cold.

4. It's over water / underground and dark.

5. "There are a lot of / a few deserts in the world," said Chris.

6. "But this is a desert with a big castle," / cave," said Cindy.

✓

 **Let's Start**

A. Write.

| Thanks |
| going to |
| Good luck |
| cousin |
| What about |
| favorite |
| anything |
| game |

1. Are you going to do _____ this weekend?

   Yes, I am. I'm _____ see my cousin.

2. How old is your _____?

   He's 14. He's my _____ cousin.

3. _____ you? What are you going to do?

   I'm going to play ice hockey. I have a _____ tomorrow.

4. _____! I hope you win. _____!

B. Look and write.

1.

   Are you going to do anything this weekend?

   No, I'm not. _____ stay home.

2.

   Are you _____?

   Yes, I am. _____ play soccer.

C. Connect and write the letter.

1. play •
2. plant •
3. go •
4. see •
5. go •
6. play •

• a play _____
• horseback riding _____
• softball __d__
• shopping _____
• ice hockey _____
• flowers _____

a.  b.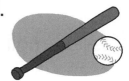

c.  d.

e.  f.

D. Write the questions and answers.

1.

What are they going to do?
They're going to play softball .

2.

What is he _____?
_____.

3.

_____?
_____.

4.

_____?
_____.

✓

Let's Learn

A. Make sentences. Then number the pictures.

1. he / rent a DVD / this weekend

   <u>He's going to rent a DVD this weekend.</u>

2. she / mail a letter / tomorrow

   _____

3. he / read a novel / next week

   _____

4. she / go backpacking / this summer

   _____

B. Look and write.

| play tennis | borrow some books | go to the zoo |

Today, May 5

1. <u>She's</u> _____

   _____

   <u>today</u> .

May 6

2. _____

   _____

   <u>tomorrow</u> .

May 13

3. _____

   _____

   <u>next week</u> .

C. Look and complete the questions and answers.

John's Week

July						
Sunday	Monday	Tuesday	Wednesday	Thursday	Friday	Saturday
4 Today!	5 mail a letter	6	7 go backpacking with friends	8	9 rent a DVD	10 borrow some books

Notes:
next week — tennis with Cheng
read novel in August

1. <u>When is he going to</u> go backpacking?

   <u>He's going to go backpacking on Wednesday</u> .

2. _____ read a novel?

   _____ .

3. _____ mail a letter?

   _____ .

4. _____ play tennis?

   _____ .

D. Look at C. Read and answer the questions.

1. Is John going to borrow some books next weekend?

   _____ .

2. Is he going to rent a DVD on Thursday?

   _____ .

3. Is he going to mail a letter this week?

   _____ .

Let's Learn More _____

A. Connect and write the sentences.

1.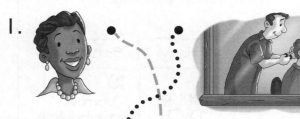

_____
_____.

2.

_____
_____.

3.

She's going to go to the
drug store .

4.

_____
_____.

5.

_____
_____.

6.

_____
_____.

department store	barber shop	drug store
supermarket	gift shop	beauty salon

B. Look and write the questions and answers.

1. Where's he going to go?

   He's _____.

2. Where's she _____?

   _____.

3. _____?

   _____.

C. Write the questions.

1.

   Is she going to go to the gift shop?

   Yes, she is.

2.

   _____?

   No, she isn't.

3.

   _____?

   Yes, he is.

Let's Build _____

Complete the conversations.

1.

Hi, Kyle! What are you doing today?

I'm staying home today.
What are _____?

I'm _____.
What are you _____ tomorrow?

_____ play softball.
I have a game.

2.

Hi, Sue. Are you _____ anything tonight?

Yes, I am. _____
_____.

Oh. What about tomorrow?
What _____?

_____ go horseback riding. Come with me!

Okay! Should I bring my jacket?

Yes. It's _____ cold.

Let's Read

A. Read and match.

1. Next summer, I'm going to go on a home stay.

2. I'm going to have an American brother and sister. Their names are Joe and Linda.

3. Two years ago, Joe stayed with my family.

4. Now, I'm going to stay with his family for two months. I have to study English every day!

B. Answer the questions.

1. What is Paul going to do? _____.

2. Who are Joe and Linda? _____.

3. Is Paul going to stay home next summer? _____.

4. When does Paul have to study English?_____.

Let's Start

A. Write.

Have fun at the park.   Why not?
Do you want to come?   What's wrong?   That's too bad.

1. Hi, Jenny. Kate and I are going to the park.
_____

2. I can't.

3. _____

4. Because I'm sick.

5. _____

6. I have a stomachache.

7. _____
I hope you feel better!

8. Thanks. _____
_____

B. Look and write.

Down

1.

2.

3.

4.

Across

5.

6.

7.

8.

C. Write the question and answer.

1. What's wrong?

   I have a _____.

2. _____?

   _____.

Let's Learn

A. Write sentences.

| paint pictures | watch sports on TV | surf the Internet |
| collect baseball cards | play badminton | write e-mail |

1.

She likes to paint pictures.

2.

_____.

3.

_____.

4.

_____.

5.

_____.

6.

_____.

B. Complete the questions and answers.

1.

What does he like to do ?
He likes to write e-mail.

2.

What does she ?
_____ play badminton.

3.

What do they ?
_____.

4.

_____?
_____.

C. Look, read, and match.

1.

• •
Does she like to collect baseball cards?
No, she doesn't.

2.
• •
Does he like to watch sports on TV?
Yes, he does.

3.
• •
Do they like to paint pictures?
No, they don't.

✓

Let's Learn More

A. Look and write.

1. He has to _____.

2. They have to _____.

3. She has to _____.

4. He has to _____.

5. She has to _____.

6. He has to _____.

| vacuum the carpet | clear the table | wash the dishes |
| take out the trash | feed the dog | dry the dishes |

B. Write the questions and answers.

1.

   What does she have to do ?

   She has to .

2.

    ?

   .

C. Circle True or False.

Chores for Sam and Lou

What do they have to do?

1. They have to take out the trash.

   (True)   False

2. They have to dry the dishes.

   True   False

3. They have to clear the table.

   True   False

4. They have to vacuum the carpet.

   True   False

5. They have to feed the dog.

   True   False

Let's Build

A. Match and complete the sentences.

1.

He has to _____,
but he wants to _____.

2.

He likes to _____,
but he doesn't like to _____.

3.

He's going to _____
tomorrow. He wants to win.

4.

He wants to _play ice hockey_,
but he has a _fever_.

5.

She wants to have fun on Friday,
but she has a _____.

B. Answer the questions.

1. Do you like to surf the Internet? _____.

2. Do you like to drink hot chocolate? _____.

3. Do you have to go to school? _____.

4. Do you have to take out the trash? _____.

Let's Read

A. Read and check.

	Serious	Easygoing
1. I have a test tomorrow. I'm not going to study.	☐	☐
2. I want to play a video game. I'm not going to do my homework.	☐	☐
3. I have some money. I'm going to save it.	☐	☐
4. I have a test tomorrow. I'm going to study.	☐	☐
5. I like to have fun!	☐	☐
6. I like to study and save my money.	☐	☐

B. Write.

What about you?

1. What are you like?

_____.

2. What is your best friend like?

_____.

3. What is your teacher like?

_____.

Units 7-8 Listen and Review

A. Read and match.

1. He's going to go horseback riding.

2. She's going to paint pictures.

3. He's going to play softball.

4. She's going to watch sports on TV.

B. Write the questions and answers.

1. What's wrong?

I have a <u>headache</u>.

2. _____?

_____.

3. _____?

_____.

C. Write the answers.

1.

Where is she going to go?

_____

2.

Where are they going to go?

_____

CHRiS AND CiNDY'S TREASURE HUNT
Part Four

A. Write.

scrapbook
adventures
camel
Carlsbad
Caverns
blank
inside
waterfall

"_____ _____ is so big," said Chris. "I feel so small."

"There's a box," said Cindy. "Let's look _____."

"It's a _____," said Cindy.

"Look! We're riding on a _____ in Egypt," said Chris.

"And we're standing in front of the _____ at Iguazu Falls," said Cindy.

"Why are there _____ pages in the scrapbook?" asked Cindy.

"Because we're going to have more _____!" said Aunt Angie.

B. Read and check.

1. Do Cindy and Chris like to travel around the world?

☐ Yes, they do.
☐ No, they don't.

2. Did Cindy and Chris find a camel in the box?

☐ Yes, they did.
☐ No, they didn't.

☐ ✓ _____

Dates

A. Write the ordinal numbers.

Sunday	Monday	Tuesday	Wednesday	Thursday	Friday	Saturday
	1st	2nd	3rd	_____	TODAY	6th
7th	_____	9th	10th		12th	_____
14th	15th	Robert's 12th Birthday	17th	18th	_____	_____
Sara's 18th Birthday	_____		24th	25th	_____	_____
28th	29th	_____	_____			

B. Look at A. Write.

1. What's the date today?_____.

2. What was the date yesterday?_____.

3. What's the date going to be tomorrow? _____.

4. When is Robert's birthday? _____.

5. When is Sarah's birthday? _____.

Outdoors

Look and write.

go to the mountains
foggy
warm
play baseball
cool
hot
play tennis
humid
go fishing
cold
go swimming
go to the beach

1. It's going to be __warm__ tomorrow. He's probably going to _play tennis_.

2. It's going to be _____ tomorrow.

   She's probably going to _____.

3. It's going to be _____ tomorrow.

   She's probably going to _____.

4. It's going to be _____ tomorrow.

   He's probably going to _____.

5. It's going to be _____ tomorrow.

   She's probably going to _____.

6. It's going to be _____ tomorrow.

   He's probably isn't going to _____.

✓

My Hopes and Dreams _____

A. Look and write.

1. Does she want to be a writer? _____.

2. Does she want to be an astronaut? _____.

3. Does she want to be a pop idol? _____.

B. What about you? Write and draw.

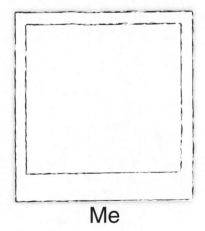

Me

1. What do you want to be?

   _____

   _____.

2. What do you want to do?

   _____

   _____.

Who's the Best?

A. Look and write.

1.

Jay   Sue   Moe

Who's the best singer?

_____.

Is Jay a better singer than Moe?

_____.

2.

Lee   Sue   Charles

Who's the worst cook?

_____.

Is Sue a worse cook than Lee?

_____.

3.

Ann   Jane   Brie

Is Jane the best runner?

_____.

Is Ann a better runner than Brie?

_____.

B. What about you? Write.

1. Are you the best dancer in your class? _____.

2. Are you the best cook in your family? _____.

3. Are you the best singer in your school? _____.

My Family and Friends

Write sentences.

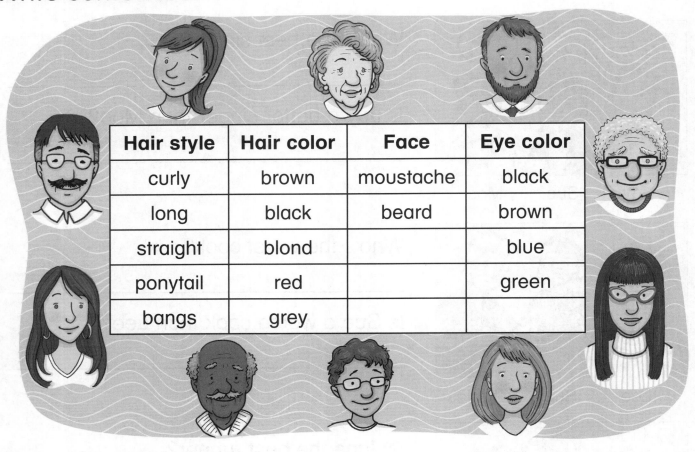

Hair style	Hair color	Face	Eye color
curly	brown	moustache	black
long	black	beard	brown
straight	blond		blue
ponytail	red		green
bangs	grey		

1. What does your mother look like?

_____.

2. What does your father look like?

_____.

3. What do you look like?

_____.

4. What does your favorite singer look like?

_____.

5. What does your teacher look like?

_____.

I'm Sick! _____

Write.

| a cold | an earache | a stomachache |
| a toothache | a cough | a sore throat |

What's wrong?

1. <u>He has a</u> _____.

2. _____.

3. _____.

4. _____.

5. _____.

6. _____.

Work and Play

A. Read and check.

1. I don't like to wash the dishes.
   It's hard.

2. I like to feed the dog.
   It's fun!

3. I don't like to paint pictures.
   It's not easy.

4. I like to watch sports on TV.
   It's great!

B. What about you? Check.

	Easy	Hard
1. vacuum the carpet	☐	☐
2. clear the table	☐	☐
3. surf the Internet	☐	☐
4. paint pictures	☐	☐
5. play badminton	☐	☐